BUSINESS STRATEGY

BRIAN TRACY

AMACOM AMERICAN MANAGEMENT ASSOCIATION
New York • Atlanta • Brussels • Chicago • Mexico City
San Francisco • Shanghai • Tokyo • Toronto • Washington, D.C.

Bulk discounts available. For details visit:
www.amacombooks.org/go/specialsales
Or contact special sales: Phone: 800-250-5308 / Email: specialsls@amanet.org
View all the AMACOM titles at: www.amacombooks.org
American Management Association: www.amanet.org

This publication is designed to provide accurate and authoritative information in regard to the subject matter covered. It is sold with the understanding that the publisher is not engaged in rendering legal, accounting, or other professional service. If legal advice or other expert assistance is required, the services of a competent professional person should be sought.

Library of Congress Cataloging-in-Publication Data

Tracy, Brian.
Business strategy / Brian Tracy.
    pages cm
Includes bibliographical references and index.
ISBN 978-0-8144-3627-1 (hardcover : alk. paper) — ISBN 978-0-8144-3628-8 (ebook) 1. Strategic planning. I. Title.
HD30.28.T72197 2015
658.4'012—dc23

                                                            2014049983

About AMA

American Management Association (www.amanet.org) is a world leader in talent development, advancing the skills of individuals to drive business success. Our mission is to support the goals of individuals and organizations through a complete range of products and services, including classroom and virtual seminars, webcasts, webinars, podcasts, conferences, corporate and government solutions, business books, and research. AMA's approach to improving performance combines experiential learning—learning through doing—with opportunities for ongoing professional growth at every step of one's career journey.

Printing number
10 9 8 7 6 5 4 3 2

CONTENTS

Introduction

WE ALL HAVE turning points in our lives, after which nothing is ever the same. When I was in my twenties, I stumbled across the subject of goals. Within thirty days my life had changed forever.

Over the years, I studied goals and learned how important they were for both business and personal success. One of the discoveries that astonished me was finding that less than 3 percent of people at all levels of business and industry have clear, specific, written, time-bounded goals for their lives that they are working toward on a daily basis.

As I began to implement goal setting in my own life and experience the remarkable changes that working toward clearly defined goals can bring about, I became interested in the subject of strategy, especially business strategy, which is really *business goal setting*. For many years, I have studied the leading military generals of history and how they used strategic thinking to achieve extraordinary victories, sometimes against overwhelming odds.

Over the last three decades, I have worked with more than 1,000 of the world's largest corporations, and over 10,000 small and medium-size businesses. I became fascinated by the subject of strategic planning and the impact it can have on an organization of any size.

What I discovered was that most companies have no strategic plan at all. What they have is a budget. They have sales projections. They have operational plans. They have hopes, dreams, and aspirations, but in terms of crystallizing the future of the organization and deciding how they are going to get from where they are to where they want to go, very few companies have a genuine strategic plan.

Business Model Innovation

We are living in an age of the most dramatic change in all of history. What worked very well for some companies for a long time does not work at all today. Companies like Blockbuster and Borders Books went from market leaders to bankruptcy in just a couple of years when the business environment changed.

Today, business model innovation is one of the hottest subjects determining business success or failure. According to the experts, fully 80 percent of companies today are attempting to survive and thrive with *obsolete* business models. Just look at what is happening to newspapers, magazines, and traditional media of all kinds. They are in serious trouble.

Your Most Important Work

What is the most important work that you do? The answer is "thinking." Your ability to think clearly about who you are, what you want, and how to create a wonderful future for your business is more important than anything else you can do. In the pages ahead, I will share with you some of the most powerful, helpful, and important ideas that have ever been developed in the subject of strategic planning. You will learn how to think better, with greater clarity, and make better decisions about the future of your business than perhaps you ever have before.

With each idea or insight, you will think of your own ideas about actions that you can take immediately to get better results. You will see things that you can change or improve in your business, starting immediately. Whether you are a one-person company or an international giant, when you and the people around you practice the principles of *Business Strategy*, you will find that you can accomplish more in a few years than organizations without this capacity are able to accomplish in five or ten years, if ever.

By thinking and acting strategically, you will increase your profitability and the level of satisfaction that you get from your company and your career. You will increase your overall levels of quality and market penetration. More than anything else, you'll have a tremendous feeling of being in control of your personal and business destiny. You will be able to look back every year or two and say, "This is exactly where we wanted to be."

ONE

Introduction to Strategy:
Alexander the Great

LET ME INTRODUCE you to the finest strategist that ever lived. In a way, he was a man who started off as a junior manager in a large organization and worked his way up. His name was Alex. Alex's father was the head of the organization and also worked his way up from the ground floor.

Alex very much admired his father, learned a lot from him, and studied under him when he was growing up. He had great dreams and aspirations of building a big organization—far bigger than the one his father oversaw.

The Alex that I am referring to is Alexander of Macedon, who became known as Alexander the Great. He was one of the first and the few men in all of human history to be called "the Great" in his lifetime and throughout the rest of history.

An Unexpected Promotion

When Alexander was 20 years old, his father was murdered. Alexander immediately became the king of Macedon.

The Macedonians were a tribe in northern Greece in what is present-day Macedonia. They were a tough, hardy, militaristic race. Under Philip, Alexander's father, they had conquered and ruled all of Greece.

Within Alexander's household, within his army and the army of his father, and among the other tribes of Greece, there were an enormous number of enemies or "market competitors" for Alexander's position. As soon as he became king, Alexander discovered that there were several plots and conspiracies internally being organized to kill him and free the city-states of Greece from Macedonian rule.

Leaders Take Command

Alexander immediately took command, as a leader does. He first of all put down the disloyal elements in his own army. He then reorganized his army quickly, put his own generals and officers in place, and then marched out and demolished the armies sent against him. As a result of these immediate and surprising victories, he became the recognized and accepted master of all of Greece, at age 21.

Alexander, like all strategic planners, had a *mission*. His was quite ambitious. He wanted to bring Greek culture to the entire known world. His long-range strategic plan was to conquer all these countries and put them under Greek rule.

Merger and Acquisition Strategy

Alexander was very smart. He did not disrupt the kingdoms that he conquered. He used the first historical version of a "merger and acquisition strategy." If they surrendered without fighting, he would leave their rulers in place. All he requested was that they pay a tribute to Greece each year, very much like a corporate income tax, and then they could go on as before. Only now, they were under the protection of the Greek empire and the Macedonians.

Alexander went even further. He would invite the soldiers of the newly conquered kingdoms to join his army and participate in the rewards that came from conquering other lands.

As Alexander moved farther south toward and through the Middle East, more and more kingdoms and tribes came and joined him. They gave up without a fight and became part of his armies. But there was still one problem.

The Major Competitor

Alexander's major competitor for world domination, the biggest empire in human history at that time, was led by Darius of Persia. This empire was enormous. It covered all of the Middle East, including the Mediterranean, and extended as far as present-day Pakistan and India. When Darius heard that a Greek army under a 22-year-old commander had invaded his empire, he was not pleased.

Darius, too, was a smart man. He recognized that Alexander was the first real threat to his power in his lifetime.

He quickly ordered an army of 50,000 to advance against Alexander's 22,000-man army. They were told to go and crush this upstart once and for all.

Alexander, anticipating that Darius would come against him, planned out a brilliant strategy and routed the army that was sent against him.

Upon hearing what had happened, Darius said, "This is serious. This is the biggest single threat to my power in my lifetime and it must be dealt with, or there will be challenges to Persian rule all over the empire."

Competitive Response

Darius was also quite competent at strategy. He sent out messengers to the dozens of different tribes throughout his empire and ordered them to send their best troops to assemble at a place called Gaugamela. He had brought together the biggest army that the world had ever seen—almost a million men. In all of history, up until World War II, there had never been an army this large assembled in one place.

When Alexander heard that Darius had assembled his massive army at Gaugamela, he immediately broke camp and marched toward the army of Darius. Alexander and his army of now 50,000 men (including soldiers from other conquered armies who had joined his ranks) arrived on the battlefield so quickly that it shocked the Persian forces, at least temporarily. Everyone knew that the next day they would be fighting one of the biggest battles in history.

The Importance of a Plan

Alexander was a great communicator. That evening, he gathered all of his commanders around his fire to explain to them exactly what he was planning to do the following day. He explained that the army of Darius was not really one single army. It was instead a whole series of small and large armies. It was made up of thirty different tribes composed of troops and levies from all over the empire, each with different languages, different cultures, different orders of battle, different religious rites, and different military structures of command. The only thing they had in common was loyalty to Darius.

Alexander believed that if something were to happen to Darius tomorrow, the rest of the armies would not stay and fight for each other; rather, they would begin to come apart, retreat, and take off in all directions. His plan: Attack into the center of the Persian defenses and kill Darius.

Take the Initiative

The day of the battle, Darius lined up his army like a massive wall of humanity—a million men to move forward to crush and overwhelm the Macedonians.

Alexander had lined up his army a little bit differently. He used a strategy that had never been seen in battle before: the "oblique formation." Instead of facing the army of Darius parallel to their front, his troops were lined up at an angle and to the right of the center of the army of Darius, giving them more maneuverability.

Then, just before the battle began, Alexander ordered his army to begin moving to the right, toward the rough terrain where his soldiers and cavalry would have an advantage and the chariots of Darius could not function.

As Alexander moved his army sideways, Darius was confused. He ordered his army to move sideways as well to maintain their front facing the Macedonians. Being ordered to shift sideways rather than to attack forward caused some confusion in the ranks of the Persian army. Then Darius ordered his first line of attack—his chariots—to charge the Macedonians; they were met with a shower of 2,000 javelins from the Macedonians, which incapacitated or destroyed half of the chariots. In all this confusion, the army of Alexander continued its rightward march. The army of Darius continued to move rightward to try to stay parallel with the forces of Alexander. Suddenly, a crack opened up in the front line of the Persian army close to where Darius was directing the battle.

Alexander saw that his critical moment was *now*. Taking advantage of the confusion and the dust cloud caused by the panicked chariots, he recognized his opportunity. He turned to his companion cavalry and said, "Come on! Let's go and kill Darius!" He then charged headlong into the center of the Persian army. This was a brilliant strategy. The only part of Darius's whole Persian army that could resist Alexander was the small contingent of troops directly facing him. All the rest of the million-man army was unable to intervene. They had no one to fight against.

Do the Unexpected

Darius was shocked. He had not anticipated this direct attack aimed squarely at him. With Alexander in the lead, the Macedonian cavalry was slashing through the front ranks of the Persians and heading straight for the command post of Darius. Darius jumped on a mare and fled from the battlefield surrounded by his senior officers.

The rest of the Persian armies had no idea what was going on amid all the dust and confusion. But the rumor went out quickly that Alexander had broken through the center of the army and that Darius had fled.

Alexander's strategy had been correct. The Persian armies began falling apart; they scattered and took off in all directions, falling over each other to get away. At this point, Alexander, who had anticipated this course of events, sent orders to his troops to begin their advance. The body of his army, known as the *phalanx*, armed with swords and spears, began to march through the Persian ranks like a hay-making machine, mowing them down by the thousands.

One Great Strategy Changed the World

By the end of the day, the Persians had lost 400,000 men. It was one of the most disastrous battles in all of human history. The Macedonians under Alexander lost 1,247 men. And Alexander, at age 23, was the undisputed master of the entire world.

The Principles of Effective Strategy

YOU MAY WONDER why I spent so much time telling you about Alexander the Great and the Battle of Gaugamela in the previous chapter. It is because the story is about an excellent strategy that led to an incredible victory that made Alexander the most powerful man in the world of his time. The military principles of strategy illustrated in the story of this battle are equally as applicable to every business, large or small.

In fact, the reason that 20 percent of businesses earn 80 percent or more of the profits in every industry is because they have a well-thought-out strategy that encompasses each of the key principles demonstrated in this battle. The absence of, or the failure to apply, a single essential strategic principle can lead to downfall and defeat of an army or a corporation, and it has—thousands of times.

The Principle of the Objective

This is the first principle of strategy. To achieve great victories, you must be clear about your goals and objectives at every level of the business. This requires that you know exactly what it is that you want to accomplish and how you are going to go about accomplishing it.

In a study reported on in *The Economist* magazine, 150 researchers spent twenty years studying 22,000 companies in a variety of countries. What they concluded was that the most efficient, effective, and profitable companies were those that took the time to set clear objectives for the company and for each person in the company. Employees knew exactly what they were expected to accomplish and when it was expected to be done. They had clear measures or benchmarks against which they could grade their progress toward the agreed-on goals.

Alexander knew exactly what he wanted to accomplish. He wanted to be the master of the entire known world. He also knew that in order to be the master of the world, he had to first of all conquer the Persian army. And the key to conquering the Persian army was to kill Darius. Both he and his entire army were absolutely clear about their objective for the battle on the plains of Gaugamela in 323 BC.

The Principle of the Offensive

Napoleon said, "No great battles are ever won on the defense."

For you to succeed in business, you must be *proactive*. You must go on the attack. You must practice the "continuous offensive" of the successful general. You must be continually moving forward with new products, new services, new processes, and new ways of doing business.

At Gaugamela, Alexander saw clearly that the only way he could defeat such a large enemy, with as much as 20-to-1 odds against him and his soldiers, was to go on the attack and never let up. This strategy enabled him to win every battle he ever fought throughout his short and glorious career.

The Principle of the Mass

All great battles are won by the general in command *massing* his forces at a critical point at a critical time to take a strategic objective.

Instead of lining up his forces across a broad front to counter the Persian army, Alexander instead kept his army together in a compact, oblique shape, at an angle to the armies of Darius. This position enabled Alexander to move his troops quickly to exploit an opportunity, which occurred when Darius allowed an opening in his front.

Even though he was outnumbered, Alexander saw that by hurling his 6,000-man companion cavalry into the heart of the army, like throwing a javelin into a target, he could completely disconcert Darius and either kill him or drive him from the field, which he did.

In business, the principle of the mass requires that you become absolutely excellent in one product niche, and dominate that niche in terms of quality and service, before you think of expanding into other products, services, or markets.

The Principle of Maneuver

In warfare, this principle refers to the importance of remaining flexible and ready to move in one direction or another no matter what the enemy does. All great battles are battles of maneuver. They are battles where the general in command uses his army skillfully, moving men and resources to those areas where they can achieve "competitive advantage."

By organizing his armies in the never-before-seen "oblique formation," Alexander was able to maintain maximum flexibility in the face of a massive enemy force. Aside from his companion cavalry at the head and center of his army, he had large cavalry units on the flanks of his forces. When Darius's forces began to break up because of the frontal attack, the rest of Alexander's army was ready to swing out in an arc and attack the entire front of the Persian army, driving it back and eventually into confusion and retreat.

The principle of maneuver applied to business refers to innovation and creativity in finding better, faster, cheaper ways to serve customers, make sales, and achieve higher levels of profitability. To maintain this kind of flexibility in business, you must always be willing to stand back and question the status quo.

The Principle of Concerted Action

This principle of military strategy requires that individuals work together like a well-oiled machine, as a team, to achieve the agreed-on goals and objectives. This is often called "cohesive unit action." It means that everyone works together cooperatively, supporting each other and bringing their resources to bear whenever and wherever they are needed to ensure that the army achieves victory.

Throughout military history, small and well-organized units have been able to defeat and destroy much larger units that were not as well coordinated. Alexander's Macedonians were perhaps the most disciplined fighting force in the world at that time. They trained exhaustively, like a top sports team. They fought as a single unit, shoulder to shoulder, reacting and responding quickly to the needs of each other in the course of fighting and winning battles.

In business, the best companies have the people with the best morale. They see themselves as part of a corporate team. They use words such as "my," "us," "we," and "our." They see the company as a natural and logical extension of themselves. They never even think "that's not my job."

The Principle of Surprise

Alexander used this device continually throughout his career to keep his opponents off balance. He never did what he was expected to do. He never attacked where he was expected to attack. He never lined up his troops or organized his forces in the face of the enemy in a way that his opponents had anticipated. He always kept them off guard.

In business, the principle of surprise means that you are always looking for ways to develop competitive advantage with products, services, processes, marketing strategies and techniques, sales methodology, and new technology to offer products and services that are new and different from anything that your competitors are offering.

The Principle of Exploitation

Once you have won the battle, gained the market, cut through the competition, and achieved a position of market dominance, you must be prepared to move rapidly to exploit it. Entrepreneur and motivational speaker Jim Rohn used to ask, "How high does a tree grow?" Answer: "As high as it can."

How much do you sell? As much as you can. Move fast. Your competitors are watching and preparing to get into your space as fast as they can. You must seize the high ground in your market and then hold on to it. Never relax.

When you get a market advantage with a superior product, service, or marketing technique, you exploit it to the fullest. You know that your competitors can copy you faster today than ever before or will do something to undermine your advantage. You cannot hesitate. You must press forward and take as much of the market as you can, while you can.

THREE

Five Questions in Strategic Planning

MANY MANAGEMENT fads come and go, with greater or lesser success. But one management skill is always the most valuable, and that is the ability to develop a clear, workable strategic plan that gives you a competitive advantage in your marketplace. There are four basic reasons why you set strategy for your business:

1. *To increase your return on equity*. It is to earn more money on the equity, or the amount of money that you have invested in your business. Equity represents ownership. It is different from return on investment (ROI) in that it represents out-of-pocket funds. The first goal of strategy, then, is to increase the amount of money you are earning on the resources that you and others have personally invested in the enterprise.

2. *To reposition your company.* You may find that your company and your products or services are under assault from your competitors. You may find, as Apple did, that you have to reposition your company with new products and new services in new markets with new technologies.

3. *To maximize your strengths and your opportunities.* Look at what it is that you do extremely well, and what your key opportunities are in the marketplace, and then move rapidly to take advantage of them.

4. *To form a basis for making action decisions now.* The whole purpose of strategy is to plan and prepare to take actions that are different from what you might have done in the absence of your new strategy.

Strategic planning is not a passive activity. Strategic planning is the process of thinking through the action steps that you are going to take to achieve your goals and objectives.

Alexander's exercises in strategy were not part of a passive or theoretical exercise. They were aimed entirely at action. Alexander was the quintessential man of action.

Five Questions to Ask and Answer

There are five key questions that you can ask and answer over and over in strategic planning. Follow this process.

ASSESS YOUR CURRENT SITUATION

Question number one is to ask yourself: *Where am I now?* Identify your business, your customers, your markets, your competitors, and your financial strengths and weaknesses. An accurate analysis of your current situation is the starting point of all strategy.

REEXAMINE YOUR PAST

Question number two is about your past. Look at your history. *How did you get to where you are today?* What were the critical steps that you took, going back a few years or even to the beginning of your business? What did you do right? What did you do wrong? What lessons did you learn? What has changed since you began in this business (recognizing that everything changes)? What were the events that got you where you are now, for better or worse?

CREATE YOUR PERFECT FUTURE

Question number three in setting strategy is to define your ideal future. *Where do you want to be in the future?* Where do you want to be one year from now, and in two, three, five, or even ten years? Where do you want to be personally, and where do you want to be as a corporation? Clearly defining your ideal future on the basis of where you are today and how you got here is critical.

PREPARE THE NEXT STEPS TO TAKE

Question number four is: *How are you going to get there?* How are you going to get from where you are today to where you want to be in the future, with the people you have, the resources you have, and the market you are working in?

My favorite exercises to answer this question are either brainstorming or mindstorming. In brainstorming, you go around the table and challenge each other to come up with at least twenty answers to the question, "What can we do to create a perfect future for this company?"

In mindstorming, you write your question at the top of a sheet of paper and then challenge yourself to generate twenty answers to that question. This is an amazing exercise for developing ideas and answers you can use to achieve any goal.

MAKE A CHECKLIST

Question number five is: *What do you need?* What additional skills, resources, or money will you require to achieve your strategic objectives sometime in the future?

One of the most powerful tools that you can use is the simple checklist. Begin to make a list of all the things that you would have to do and all the steps you would have to take to get from where you are today to where you want to be at some time in the future.

Brilliant on the Basics

When Vince Lombardi became the head coach of the Green Bay Packers in 1959, he was asked what he was going to change or do differently. He replied that he was not going to change the players, the plays, or the training schedule. Instead, they were going to become "brilliant on the basics."

To be successful in strategic planning and in business, you must become brilliant on the basics of strategic planning, and you do that by continuing to ask and answer the right questions.

FOUR

The Key Players in Setting Strategy

ONE OF THE FIRST questions I'm asked whenever I'm organizing a strategic planning session for a company is, "Who should attend?"

The simplest answer is that everyone who will be *responsible* for implementing the strategy should be involved in the process of setting the strategy in the first place.

It is essential that the CEO, the CFO, the chairman, or whoever will be ultimately responsible for the implementation of the strategy be in attendance the entire time. This is the person who must sign off on the strategy, give his or her approval to the strategy, and make the final decisions necessary to allocate time, people, and resources to the implementation of the strategy.

The Power of the President

Some time ago, I conducted a three-day strategic planning session for a large oil company. The president of the company sat in and attended every minute of that three-day process. He carefully listened to what everyone had to say and offered his observations and comments as the days passed.

By the end of the three days, there was cohesion and a commitment of all the people around the table to the company, to each other, and to the success of the strategic plan that they had mutually developed. The company has since gone on to become one of the largest and most profitable companies in the world.

A Failure of Leadership

In another situation, the president of a billion-dollar company brought me in to conduct a strategic planning session. However, the chairman, who was a descendent of the founding family and who had the power to agree or disagree with anything the executives came up with, refused to attend the session. He didn't think it was a good use of his time.

During an intensive and enjoyable three-day stay at a resort, we developed a strategic plan for this large national company that was quite excellent. The implementation of this plan would give this company a competitive advantage in a challenging marketplace. Everyone in the strategic planning session was excited about the plan and committed to making it a reality.

Lack of Support

But afterward, when the company president explained the new plan to the chairman, the person with the final authority to approve or disapprove of the plan, he dismissed it as being "largely a waste of time." He told the president that he was quite capable of making all the strategic decisions necessary for the future of this national corporation. When word of his reaction got out, all the enthusiasm toward the implementation of this strategic plan died away, like the air being let out of a balloon. The company went back to "doing the same old things in the same old way."

A few years later, this dynamic company—highly admired and respected by its customers and competitors—foundered in the sea of vigorous competition and eventually went bankrupt.

Who Will Implement the Plan?

The next group of people who need to be involved in strategic planning are the *implementers* of the strategy. They are the key players whose cooperation and involvement will be required. They are usually the senior executives of the organization, the people in charge of the major departments and functions. The more involved they are in the setting of the strategy, the more likely it is that the strategy will be implemented effectively.

There is a simple rule in human interaction: There is a direct relationship between the amount of time that people spend discussing and asking questions about a course of action and their degree of commitment to carrying out whatever decisions are made. The more you talk about a course of action, encourage input, ask and answer questions, and stimulate discussion, the more dedicated each person will be to making the strategy a success.

You Need Outside Help

Strategic planning is something you cannot do by yourself. It's like dentistry or medical work or the law. You have to get someone who is objective, who has knowledge and exposure to different industries, and who has studied in and is experienced in strategic planning.

You need someone who can come in and be a facilitator of the strategic planning process. This person will take the time to fully understand your company, your people, your markets, your competition, and the situation you are facing in your business today. As they say, "A person who acts as his own lawyer has a fool for a client."

A person who tries to be his own strategic planner probably has a fool for a client as well.

Even I use an outside strategic planner when I am doing strategic planning for my own business.

Create the Right Environment

A good strategic planning exercise requires two to four days of committed, unbroken time. It is best done in a "place apart," where there are no interruptions and where people can completely change their mental space.

One of the best places is a resort away from the city, where there are no distractions. The quality of the thinking and the contributions of each person will be in direct proportion to the amount of time that the executives present can focus and concentrate on the future of the business.

FIVE

Values, Vision, and Purpose

THERE IS A SAYING in business that "before you do anything, you have to do something else first."

In strategic planning, what you have to do first is think about and agree on the foundation principles of your business.

The starting point is your thinking through the *values* that you stand for and believe in. What are they?

Your values are the foundation principles of your business. They tell you what you stand for and what you will not stand for. They give you guidance and direction in decision making and in everything you do in your business.

The Fortunate 500

When Norman Vincent Peale and Ken Blanchard put together what they called "the Fortunate 500" in their book, *The Power of Ethical Management*, they reported that those companies that had clear, written values and principles that everyone knew and shared were consistently more profitable than companies that may have had values but didn't write them down or widely share them.

Most successful companies in America are those that are crystal clear about their values. The most successful men and women in the world seem to be those whose values are clear to them. They refuse to compromise them for any short-term gain or advantage.

IBM is an excellent example. It has consistently been rated as one of the most admired companies in the world. From the founding of IBM by Thomas J. Watson Sr., the values of IBM have always been "excellent products, excellent customer service, and respect for the individual." The company has been organized around those three principles since 1928. Its success and esteem in the world marketplace is testimony to how closely it adheres to those values.

What Are Your Values?

When we conduct a strategic planning session, the first thing we do is to get agreement or consensus on the values that the company believes in, the order of those values in terms of priority, and how those values are actually lived out or practiced in the day-to-day activities of the business.

Some of the most common values espoused by companies are *integrity, quality, customer service, innovation, entrepreneurship*, and *profitability*, among others.

Ask yourself: What are your company values? Do you value quality? Do you believe in product or service excellence? Do you believe in taking care of people? Do you believe in market leadership or innovation? What are your fundamental beliefs about what is right and wrong?

What Would Others Say?

If you were to survey the people in your company and ask them what values your company stood for and believed in, what would people say? Would there be clarity and unanimity among your employees about your company values? Or would there be contradictions and disagreements?

What if you surveyed your customers and asked them, "What are the fundamental values of this company?" What would your customers say?

Your values are only and always expressed in your *actions,* your behaviors on a day-to-day and minute-to-minute basis, especially *under pressure.* You can really tell what a person or an organization believes in and stands for by looking at what they do and how they behave in a crisis, large or small. This is the "testing time" of the values of a person or an organization.

Values Create a Strong Foundation

One of my clients, as a start-up, needed to decide the values upon which the company would be based. The executive team came together and selected five values, starting with integrity and ending with profitability. They then agreed on a one-sentence statement of how each value would be practiced throughout the company. These value statements were then printed on plasticized cards and handed out to everyone. They became the basic operating principles of the company. Every time the executives in the company had to make a decision, they would take out their "values cards" and discuss how they should act based on the values that they had committed to.

Within a few years, this company became one of the leading organizations in the industry, even though it faced tremendous entrenched competition.

What Is Your Vision?

Once you are clear about your values, you then take some time to project into the future. You develop a vision for what your company would look like if it was perfect in every way. I sometimes like to talk about vision as a "five-year fantasy." What is yours?

In its simplest terms, the most effective overall vision for a company is to "be the best." It is to be excellent in products, services, and customer relations. It is to be the top company in terms of leadership and management, the people who work in the business, and its reputation with customers and the market in general.

Peter Drucker once said that even when a business is starting out at a kitchen table, if the business does not dream of world leadership, it will never be a big success. Your dream should be of world leadership as well. If this were true, what actions would you have to begin taking immediately to achieve this exciting vision of tomorrow?

What Would Customers Say?

What is your ideal vision of your customer toward you? How do you want your customers to think about your company? Looking at your company from the outside, from the perspective of customers working with you, being involved with your people, using your products and services, and then turning around and talking about you to other people, how would you like them to describe your company? This is an excellent starting point for determining what your values and vision should be.

Theodore Levitt of the Harvard Business School said that the most valuable asset a company has is its *reputation*. A company's reputation is defined as "how it is known to others."

Your reputation is determined by what customers, competitors, suppliers, outside vendors, and the general public say about you when they discuss your company, your products, and your services among themselves.

What are they saying about you today? What would you like them to be saying about you and your company in the future? What could you do, starting today, to ensure that people both outside and inside your company think about you and talk about you in a particular way?

Be a Fly on the Wall

Imagine the people in your company describing your business to other people. What would your staff tell others about the kind of company they work for? What kind of working climate do you provide? What kind of people work in your company? What kind of an organization have you developed? What would be your ideal view if you could have your company described with any words at all?

Finally, how do you get from where you are now, the way you are currently perceived by other people, to the way that you would like to be perceived at some time in the future? Especially, how would it be useful for you to be described to others? What kind of description of your business would be most helpful for growing your business and working toward market leadership?

Determine Your Purpose

Your purpose is your reason "why." Why do you do what you do? What purpose does your business serve in the great scheme of things? What difference do you make in the lives of others, especially your customers and staff?

Nietzsche wrote, "A man can bear any what if he has a big enough why."

Your purpose in life or business is almost always defined in terms of what you do to improve or enrich the lives or work of other people.

Your purpose flows naturally out of clarity about your values and your vision. It enables you to explain to yourself and to others what is important to you and what motivates you in life.

SIX

Determine Your Corporate Mission

ONCE YOU HAVE decided upon your values, vision, and purpose for your business, the next step is for you to determine your mission.

Mission is an essential part of all business strategy.

Alexander's mission was clear. It was to bring Greek culture and civilization to all of the known world. To achieve this mission, he knew he would have to overcome tremendous resistance to succeed.

For you to achieve business success, you will have to overcome tremendous competitive resistance as well. To achieve the market success you desire, clarity is essential. You must be clear about your values, your vision, your mission, and your purpose.

Define It Qualitatively

A mission statement is always *qualitative*, not quantitative. A mission statement is not to "Earn a lot of money" or "Increase profitability." A mission statement is directed outward, toward what you want to do to help and improve the lives of your customers.

GE's mission statement is: "General Electric is a unique, high-spirited, entrepreneurial enterprise known for its unmatched level of excellence, highly profitable with world-wide leadership in each of its product lines."

With this mission statement as a driving force behind the activities of the company, General Electric has gone on to become one of the most successful businesses in history. Under Jack Welch, and today under Jeffrey Immelt, GE has become a world leader in innovative products and services, business growth, and profitability, and has the respect and esteem of almost everyone who knows the company.

Your Umbrella Statement

A mission statement is often referred to as your "umbrella statement." It is the organizing principle under which everything in the company is done. The mission statement tells people what the company does, and also what the company does not do.

A good mission statement contains both a method and a measure. Just as a mission is something that can be accomplished, you must have clear measures and standards that you can use to determine how close you are to achieving your mission.

A simple format for a mission statement could be: "Our mission is to (describe how you intend to improve the life or work of your customers). We achieve this mission by (the methods you will use), and we measure how successful we are by (insert the exact numbers that you will achieve if you are successful in completing your mission)."

Example:

Our mission is to be the best provider of our product or service to our market, enabling our customers to enjoy enormous improvements in their work and personal lives. Our method is to continually increase product quality and to aggressively market to newer and better customers. We measure our success by growing 20 percent or more each year in sales and profitability.

Make It Clear

A good mission statement should be clear, specific, measurable, and capable of being both understood and embraced by everyone responsible for achieving the mission. By this measure, most mission statements are vague and unclear. They do not give guidance and direction to people in the company, and no one has any idea when or whether the mission has been achieved or how close you are to accomplishing it.

In times of turbulence and rapid change, it is often a good idea to revisit your mission statement. It may be partially or totally obsolete. Your products, services, markets, customers, and technology may have changed dramatically. Your mission statement must keep up with the times.

Sometimes, revisiting and rewording a mission statement can change the direction of your business. It can lead to new decisions, new strategies, and new actions. Your values of integrity, quality, and customer service excellence, combined with your vision of being the best in your industry, can remain the same. But your mission may have to change or be updated in the face of new realities.

The Right Combination

Establishing a mission statement is like getting the right combination to a lock. Once you have the right combination and you turn to the right numbers in the right sequence, the lock will open. The actual strategy will begin to formulate itself as the step-by-step process by which you accomplish the mission.

SEVEN

Back from the Future

STRATEGY IS THE path that takes your company to the ideal future. Strategic planning starts with knowing where you are now, envisioning your ideal future, then focusing on what needs to change in the present to create the future.

What Is Your Business?

Before you can decide where you want to go, you have to know with complete clarity where you are today.

Start by asking: What is your business today? Describe it clearly. Describe it in terms of what your product or service actually does to change or improve the life of your customers.

Many people are not quite sure what their business actually is. A good example comes from the history of the railroads. The railroad companies used to think that their business was running railroads when their business was really transporting goods and services.

Most of the railroads in the United States eventually went bankrupt or nearly bankrupt because most of the shipping of people, goods, and services was taken over by trucking, airplanes, and ships.

As a counterexample, in Canada there is a company called Canadian Pacific Railway. It recognized early on that its business was transportation of all kinds. With this insight, the company expanded into Canadian Pacific Airlines, Canadian Pacific Trucking, Canadian Pacific Shipping, and other modes of transportation. Whatever you want to send (including yourself) by any mode of transportation, Canadian Pacific has a solution for you.

Look at the Numbers

Conduct a current analysis of yourself and your business. Where are you now? What are your sales and profit margins? What are your prices and costs?

What about your financial results? What are your sales and profit margins? What are your prices and costs? Look at your sales figures and break them down by product, product line, service, market, and distribution channel. What are your financial strengths and weaknesses? What are the resources that you have available?

Next, look at your sales targets and compare them with your results. Are sales meeting your expectations? Are your sales trending upward or downward? If downward, what can you do to turn them around? If upward, are you convinced that they will continue to increase? What are your prices and costs?

Now focus on your profits and your profit margins. Ask the same questions. Are they meeting expectations? Are they trending upward or downward?

What's Your Return?

Analyze your products and services. Which are selling well? Which are the most profitable? Which are selling poorly? On which products are you losing money? One of the traps that many companies fall into is to continue to sell popular products or services on which they're losing money. The goal of your business is not to sell lots of products, but to make money. If you're losing money on every product you sell, selling more products only means you're losing more money.

Look at your return on sales. Also look at your return on investment and return on equity. Are they increasing or decreasing? Are you making the right decisions?

The Customer Is King

What is your return on customer? Just as you can lose money on every product, you can lose money on every customer. These are not the customers that you want to sell to. Who are your least profitable and most profitable customers today? You want to eliminate your least profitable customers and keep your best customers.

What makes your customers happy? Why do your best customers keep coming back? What do they like most about what you do for them? Understanding your number one area of customer satisfaction is key.

Be brutally honest and also look at what your customers don't like. What's the number one reason for customer complaints? What are you not offering that sends customers and potential customers to your competitors?

Your Market Position

Understanding your position in the market means recognizing your own strengths and weaknesses. What does your company do very well? What are your vulnerabilities? What is your position in the market? Who are your main competitors? How do you rank in comparison with your competitors? Who are your secondary competitors?

What are your competitors doing right? What are their strengths and weaknesses? What are you doing better or worse than them?

Go through every detail and again be brutally honest. Harold Geneen of the conglomerate ITT said, "Get the facts. Get the real facts. Not the apparent facts, the hoped-for facts, or the obvious facts. Get the real facts based on analysis. Facts don't lie."

Where Do You Want to Go?

Once you fully understand where you are now, the next question to examine is where you want to be in the future.

Looking at current trends, where is your business going? Where will it be in two or three years? Will it grow, decline, or continue on its present path? Knowing that the future will always be different from the present, where is your business heading on its current trajectory?

Consider the Possibilities

Ask yourself: What could this business be tomorrow?

What are the possibilities for your business? What could you do differently, or what new areas could you go into that would change your business? What new products and services could you develop and sell, and in what different ways and places?

Imagine No Limitations

Then ask: What *should* it be? What should your business be three to five years from now? If you could wave a magic wand and create an absolutely wonderful business, and if you had no limitations, what could or should your business be like at some time in the future?

I once conducted a strategy session for a multibillion-dollar company that was in trouble. New competition and new government regulations had plunged the company into a state of chaos, leading to layoffs, downsizings, and divestments. I started the session with a process that I call "idealization." The goal was to get the company's executives to stop focusing on the present and instead focus on an ideal future. I told the top managers around the table to create a "five-year fantasy."

A five-year fantasy is an exercise that will help you imagine an ideal future. To create this fantasy in detail, ask yourself a series of questions: How big would your company be? What kind of reputation would it have? What products and services would you be offering that enabled you to dominate your market? What kind of people would work for your company, and what kind of leadership would you have? What level of profitability would you be achieving? How high would your stock price be?

When I went through the exercise with the managers of the company in trouble, we ended up with twenty-seven different descriptions of the ideal company, which we then converted into clear goals. These goals included, among others, highly profitable, great market reputation, high stock price, high growth rate, top leadership, fabulous customer service, and a great place to work. Every one of the managers present said they believed that all of the goals could be achieved within five years.

Back-from-the-Future Thinking

Once you have clearly described your ideal future, go back to your present situation and decide what you have to do, starting today, to turn your vision of the ideal future into reality. This is called "back from the future" thinking. Make a list of everything that needs to happen to realize the five-year fantasy. This is the beginning of creating your strategic plan.

EIGHT

Strategic Areas for Consideration

THE BASIC STRATEGIC variables for consideration as you make a plan for the future are *products, services, customers, markets, finances, people, technology,* and *production capability.* These are the areas of your business that you may continue as before or change, depending on your strategic goals.

Products and Services

What exactly are the products and services that you are planning to offer? What do they do to change or improve the lives or work of your customers? What is it about them that makes them clearly superior and the best choice for the customers that you are going after?

Customers

Who is your ideal customer, your *perfect* customer? What are the *demographics* of your ideal customer? What is this customer's age, education, income, occupation, and level of family formation?

What are your customers' *psychographics*? What are their goals, ambitions, desires, and aspirations? What are their fears, misgivings, or suspicions that might cause them to hesitate from buying your product or service?

Especially, what are their *ethnographics*? What do they use your product or service for? How do they use it? How does it change or improve their lives in some way?

In the past, you chose your product, then sought out customers. In many cases today, however, companies are identifying the customer and the customer's exact needs and then retrofitting or reverse engineering product and service development based on what the customer says he or she wants. Companies are moving from "product development" to "customer development" and not even creating the product until the customer has agreed to buy it at a particular price.

Markets

What markets are you going to enter? How are you going to penetrate these markets? Are you going after geographic markets, horizontal markets, or vertical markets? Who are your competitors in these markets? How do you need to advertise, promote, sell, and otherwise penetrate these markets?

Finances

How much money do you have, and how much money will you need to achieve and sustain profitability?

People

Who are the key people you will need in terms of skills, abilities, and proven competence? Where and how will you get and keep these people?

Technology

What sort of technology will you require to build and operate your business? Is your current technology sufficient and satisfactory in light of the rapid changes in technology that your competitors are adapting?

Production Capability

Finally, what is your production capability? How much can you produce, deliver, sell, and service in a competent fashion? What do your products or services cost to produce, sell, deliver, install, and service?

Set Clear Goals

A few years ago, *Fortune* magazine reported on a study that was done to determine why so many CEOs were being let go from Fortune 500 companies. The most important reason cited was "failure to execute." The CEOs had been placed in their positions with clear, specific performance expectations for their respective companies. In each case, the executive had not achieved the goals and objectives laid out from the start.

Every month, you hear or read about top executives who are dismissed by their corporations because of the failure to achieve the key objectives of sales and profitability for which they were responsible. Lack of clarity about what those objectives actually were is almost always a major factor in the failure to achieve those objectives over time.

Successfully leading your company's strategy depends on your having the same laserlike focus on goals. You cannot implement your strategy if you do not have absolute clarity on the strategic goals of the company.

What is your main objective for your business or for your position? What are you trying to do? How are you trying to do it? Could there be a better way? Are your goals and objectives realistic based on the current situation? What are your assumptions? What if your assumptions are wrong? What would you do then?

As Peter Drucker said, "Errant assumptions lie at the root of every failure."

Always be open to the possibility that you could be doing the wrong thing. Your business model may be obsolete. What seemed like a good decision at one time, in one or more of these areas, is no longer a good decision today.

NINE

The Driving Force:
Key to Strategy

THE IDEA OF THE driving force can help you think with greater clarity about the present and future of your business, and everything you do.

The term *driving force* comes courtesy of business consultants John Zimmerman and Benjamin Tregoe and is a major concept in strategy. Once adopted, the driving force becomes the quantitative principle around which all planning is done.

There are several driving forces that you can choose from. But there is always one that becomes the most important organizing principle of your business.

Here's an important point. Just because you have, for example, a product-driven driving force for your business does not mean that you are not also focused on other areas of customer need and customer satisfaction. Your driving force is the "point of the spear" in all of your thinking about your business, your customers, and your financial results.

The Product or Service Driving Force

The product or service driving force determines the scope of your markets and the range of your products. Let us say that you are a Domino's Pizza or a McDonald's. You would then have a product-driven driving force. The focus of your strategy and everything in your organization would be to sell more of your product to ever more customers in as many different ways as possible.

If you were an accounting or legal firm, you would have a service-driven driving force. Your goal would be to sell more of your specific services to more customers in as many different ways as possible.

The Market Needs Driving Force

This driving force exists when you identify a particular market and you ask yourself, "What is it that my market needs and wants?" You then develop the products or services for that specific market.

One of my clients has been All-State Legal Supply. It is an excellent company with a very clear focus. It is an all-purpose firm that provides everything that a law office needs to operate efficiently from the time it signs its lease to the time it closes its doors. This company supplies furniture, computers, software, stationery and office supplies, and even temporary services when necessary.

Technology-Driven Driving Force

This driving force occurs when you build your business around your technology. One prime example of a technology-driven driving force company is Apple. Apple does not produce refrigerators or sell groceries. Apple only manufactures products where its advantages and innovations in technology can give it market advantages over competitors.

Whether you are in computers, software, Internet marketing, telecommunications equipment, and so on, your technology will determine the products and services you offer, the markets you serve, and the new products that you would develop.

Production Capability Driving Force

In this case, your production capability would determine the products and services you offer and the markets that you aim at. For example, a furniture manufacturing company's driving force would be to create more and better varieties of furniture that it can sell to more customers in more markets.

IKEA would be a perfect example of a production capability driving force company. Everything it does is to design and produce more varieties of easy-to-assemble furniture for more and more people in ever-expanding markets. It has the equipment—the lathes, drills, and assembly lines—for manufacturing furniture and furniture components. Its production capability determines how much and what kind of furniture it can make.

The Method of Sales Driving Force

In this case, it is your method of sales that determines your products, services, and all of your business activities. Sales methods could be retail, wholesale, direct mail, Internet, distributors, or manufacturer's representatives.

In our business and in millions of other businesses worldwide today, the method of sales is digitally downloaded products sold via the Internet and delivered online. Because our method of sales is to contact prospective customers and offer them our knowledge-based digital products, this determines the entire structure of our business, from product development through to technology requirements, staffing, office facilities, marketing, sales, pricing, customer relationships, and everything else.

The Method of Distribution Driving Force

Sometimes your method of distribution determines the products or services that you offer, and the way that you offer them. For example, Avon distributes products by demonstrating its cosmetics to women both individually and in groups. This face-to-face method of distribution determines the entire structure of the company, including what new products Avon will offer, how those products will be priced, sold, and delivered, and the company's entire reimbursement and financial structure.

The Natural Resources Driving Force

For companies like ExxonMobil, Weyerhaeuser, Shell, or British Petroleum, the driving force would be natural resources extraction, processing, shipping, and delivery, whether oil, gas, coal, timber, or various minerals like copper, gold, or iron ore. The location of natural resources and the customers or markets for those natural resources determine everything that the company does.

The Size/Growth Driving Force

For many companies, their driving force can be their goals for growth in sales and profitability. For many years, Toyota has had a size/growth driving force. The carmaker's objective has been to gain market share. As it gained more market share, because of the economies of scale of manufacturing, Toyota's costs of production decreased and its profitability increased.

The Return/Profit Driving Force

Many companies, especially those with multiple product/service lines, use return/profit as their driving force. They will purchase or start a company or enter into any market where they can earn excellent profits.

American Home Products was famous for this strategy for many years. It offered a variety of different products and services for individuals, corporations, businesses, and families throughout the country. The company had one simple driving force: Every single product must yield a 20 percent pretax return on sales. If a product does not have that kind of profitability, then a company driven by return/profit won't carry it or will quickly abandon it.

Determine Your Driving Force

What is your driving force? What is your primary driving force, and what are your secondary driving forces? The selection of your driving force is absolutely essential to your business future.

Because you select a single driving force, which you must do if you are going to focus and concentrate on maximizing sales and profitability in your industry, it doesn't mean that you don't have other forces operating as well. It just means that the driving force you select becomes the primary organizing principle of your business.

TEN

Four Central Concepts in Strategic Planning

THERE ARE FOUR strategic planning principles in business that are timeless. Success or failure in any one of these four areas can lead to dramatic changes in business results, for better or for worse. We discuss these principles in great detail in my seventh book in this series, *Marketing*.

Know Where to Specialize

The first is *specialization*. Today, we live in a world where we have to specialize and do a few things exceptionally well. Your chosen area of specialization largely determines the future of your business.

You can specialize in a product or service, a customer segment, or a market area. When you specialize in a product or service area, your specialization is easy to describe. When asked, "What kind of business are you in?" your immediate answer will be "life insurance," or "orthopedic surgery," or "seafood restaurants," or "enterprise software," and so on.

Choose Your Market

Another possible area of specialization has to do with your market. You can specialize in a particular type of customer. For example, in my business as a professional business speaker, I engage with the managers and executives of corporations, on the one hand, and the owners of small and medium-size enterprises (SMEs), on the other hand, no matter where they are located. I work worldwide and have spoken in sixty-seven countries. I've written seventy books and produced several hundred audio and video learning programs. But these materials are all aimed at managers and executives on the one hand and entrepreneurs and business owners on the other. This is where I specialize.

You can specialize in a geographic area. A convenience store will specialize in a single neighborhood. A manufacturer can specialize in satisfying the demand for its product worldwide. But in every case, you must specialize and be clear about your area of specialization.

Be Different from Your Competitors

The second concept in strategic planning is *differentiation*. All marketing is differentiation. All selling is differentiation. All business requires that you differentiate your product or service so that it appears superior to that of your competitors and is viewed as a better choice.

Peter Drucker once said, "The purpose of marketing is to make selling unnecessary." Apple is a perfect example. When Apple announces a new product or service, people line up around the block and sleep on the street to be the first purchasers. They do not need to be sold. Because Apple's quality reputation is so excellent, people are "sold" by the very announcement of a new product.

Competitive Advantage

Another term for differentiation is "competitive advantage." Sometimes we refer to your area of differentiation as your "area of excellence." Michael Porter of Harvard Business School refers to the need to develop a source of "unique added value" that offers your customers something that they value and are willing to pay for, and that no other competitor can offer.

What is your competitive advantage? What makes your products or services superior to those of your competitors? What is the unique added value that your customers receive when they buy from you that no one else can offer? Your ability to ask and answer these questions is perhaps the most important part of business strategy.

Select Your Ideal Customer

The third principle of marketing strategy is *segmentation*. Many marketing experts believe that all marketing today is segmentation. This is the development of absolute clarity about those specific customers who most appreciate the qualities of your product or service in your area of specialization.

We referred to segmentation in Chapter Eight when we asked the question, "Who exactly is your perfect customer?" The answer to this question is the person who most appreciates your area of specialization and most desires the unique added value that you offer. Your ideal customer is the one who will buy the fastest and has the least price resistance.

One strategy is to identify your target market, your perfect customer, then to focus single-mindedly on being the superior choice of the people in that market segment in the product or service category that you represent.

Another strategy, if you are not selling as much as you want to your current customers, is to *change your customer*. Find or develop a new customer who will better appreciate the special qualities of your product or service offerings.

The greater clarity you have in describing the ideal customer for your business, the easier it is for you to organize all of your advertising and promotion so that it is aimed at precisely the customer you want to attract and who will most appreciate what you offer.

Focus and Concentrate

The fourth strategic principle of marketing is *concentration*. Once you specialize, differentiate, and segment, you can then dedicate 100 percent of your resources to focusing and concentrating on the best and most profitable potential customers for your business.

Once you have developed an excellent product or service and clearly identified the very best customers who can and will buy your product/service at prices that are profitable for you, you then concentrate single-mindedly on dominating that market segment.

Or, as Alexander said to his troops at the Battle of Gaugamela, "Kill Darius. Kill Darius. Kill Darius."

ELEVEN

Concentrate on What You Do Well

IN DISCUSSING military strategy, we talked about the principle of the mass—that is, the ability of the general to bring all of his forces to concentrate in a single place at a single time to achieve victory, often against overwhelming odds. You can do the same.

Bill Gates Jr., Warren Buffett, and Bill Gates Sr. were at a dinner party. While they were chatting, one of the guests came up to them and asked this question: "You gentlemen are some of the most successful people in the world. What would you say is the most important quality for success today?"

The three men broke off their conversation, turned to the dinner party guest, and replied, simultaneously, "Focus!"

All three agreed that the ability to focus single-mindedly on one thing at a time was absolutely essential to success in a world of ceaseless activity and turbulence, constant and never-ending distractions, and so many demands for the attention of each person. Focus is the key.

The 80/20 Rule Revisited

When we talk about concentration of power or *focus*, we think again about the 80/20 rule. This rule says that 20 percent of the things you do will account for 80 percent of your results. This rule, which goes back to Vilfredo Pareto in 1895 and is now called the "Pareto principle," was true then and it is true now.

Because you cannot do everything, you need to concentrate on those few things that you can do well and that represent the greatest potential for business and financial results. All business strategy revolves around massing your powers. You need to focus and leverage your strengths to achieve maximum advantage in the marketplace.

Profit from the Core

In Chris Zook and James Allen's excellent book, *Profit from the Core*, the authors show that successful companies are those that dominate a core market that is highly profitable and then expand carefully into only those nearby markets where they already have a high level of knowledge and experience.

Their point is that the 80/20 rule seems to apply. Eighty percent of your profits come from the 20 percent of products or services that you offer in an excellent fashion, while 80 percent of your business activities will account for only 20 percent of your profits. You must always be studying your business and asking yourself, "What are the 20 percent of my activities that account for 80 percent of the value of all of my activities?"

What are your most profitable products and services? What are they today? What could they be tomorrow? Who are your most important and valuable customers today? Who could be your best customers tomorrow, and how could you attract and keep more of them?

One of the biggest weaknesses that we have in business today is the tendency to "scatter our forces." As Jack Trout said in *The Power of Simplicity*, "One of our biggest business problems is that we offer too many products and services at too many different price points, to too many different customers in too many different markets."

When Steve Jobs returned to Apple in 1996, the company was producing 104 different products and was in serious financial trouble. The company had only enough cash to last for another ninety days. One of the first things that Jobs did was announce that Apple was discontinuing 100 of those 104 products, as quickly as possible. By doing so, he freed up financial resources and personnel (engineers and developers) to focus on the "next big thing," which turned out to be the iPod.

The rest is history. Within a few years, Apple was the most valuable company in the world.

Focus and concentration on your greatest opportunities and areas of highest profit potential have always been the keys to financial success in business.

Distinctive Capabilities

New research from Northwestern University's Kellogg School of Management shows that focusing on one thing that you do well—supported by what the researchers call "distinctive capabilities"—is the new path to competitive advantage.

In the old days, the leading companies were conglomerates with a simple "get big and get powerful" strategy: They piled up assets and used their size and reach to build unbeatable economies of scale. Then they'd go find short-term growth and profitability wherever they could find within their huge operations.

Conglomerate power is not the strategy of today's best companies. "They do not follow the traditional portfolio strategies of seeking short-term profitability or growth wherever they can find it," the Kellogg researchers wrote in the August 2014 edition of *Strategy + Business* magazine. "Rather, they recognize that value is created by their distinctive capabilities: what they can do consistently well."

Amazon does three things well: world-class information technology, distribution of products, and an automated customer recommendation system. Those capabilities are the pillars on which the Amazon empire was built.

Apple also does just three things well: insight into what consumers want, consumer-friendly designs, and technological integration. Technological integration means the ability to get products to work together—so your iPhone can connect to your computer, for example. Those three things were all that was needed for Apple to revolutionize how we use our phones and how we listen to music.

Where should you be concentrating your time, money, and resources today to succeed greatly in today's market? Whatever your answer, don't delay. Do it now. As Winston Churchill said, "If you do not act when you have a chance of victory, soon you will have to act when you have no chance at all."

TWELVE

Adjacency Moves

THE BEST STRATEGY is to focus on what you do well, and to concentrate on just a few core businesses based on core capabilities. To grow your company, you will need to expand beyond the core business. Many companies fall into the trap of expanding into businesses that are too far away from their core activities. They don't have the experience, the capabilities, or the brand name to succeed.

In *Beyond the Core*, his follow-up book to *Profit from the Core*, Chris Zook explains that companies need to grow by moving into adjacency areas—areas that build on the capabilities of the core business.

Three Truths
Walmart opened up the Sam's Club large-volume discount stores. American Airlines developed the Sabre automated

flight reservation system. Nike moved from shoes to sportswear. Enterprise Rent-A-Car's expansion was from leasing cars to renting cars to dealerships. All are examples of adjacency moves that built on core businesses.

Not all adjacency moves are successful. While Walmart expanded beyond its traditional stores, Kmart's adjacency expansions into retail stores for books and for sporting goods were failures.

According to Zook, adjacency strategies will be successful if they follow three truths:

1. They are built on the strongest cores of the companies.

2. They have a repeatable characteristic.

3. They involve the strong customers.

A repeatable formula is one of the most powerful elements of the adjacency strategy. Nike moved into one sport, then another, then another, always following the same pattern. The repeatable formula in most cases is built on insights into customers that can be applied to different products or customer segments. These insights include understanding and evaluating the cost and profit economics of customers, purchasing related to life cycle events, and share-of-wallet opportunities. Share-of-wallet strategies can be particularly successful. If customers are buying this one product from your company, why wouldn't they buy this very related second product from you?

Profit Pools

As you are bringing your customers into adjacency areas, it's important that those areas represent a significant profit pool, Zook says. In other words, there is a great potential for profit. When IBM moved from product-orientation to services with the creation of IBM Global Services, it realized that as compared with hardware sales, information technology services represented a greater chance for high profits. Where are your untapped profit pools? Are they closely related to what you do well in your core business?

Be careful about blundering into what looks like an attractive profit pool in which you have little chance of success. Before moving ahead, ask yourself these questions:

- Are you mistaking a large market for a large profit pool?

- Is the profit pool controlled by a powerful incumbent? Are you underestimating the strength of this market leader?

- Do you understand the root cause of market power in that profit pool?

- Are you underestimating how competition in the profit pool might shift in the future?

Speed is important, but haste is going to make waste. Do your homework. Don't make unsupported assumptions. Don't underestimate the hurdles.

THIRTEEN

Have a Divestment Strategy

A STRATEGY IS successful if it focuses your efforts and time on what you do very well. Strategic planning is not only about what you need to *start* doing based on your strategy choices. It's also about what you need to *stop* doing.

Remember, to start something new, you must stop doing something old. Your *dance card is full.* Your resources are already taxed to the full, if not overtaxed. To do something new in the future, you must free up time and resources by discontinuing things that you are doing today.

Divestment strategy means that you have to get rid of yesterday before you can go on to tomorrow. What are you going to get out of, cut back on, remove, or eliminate altogether? One of the basic rules in strategic thinking is to never go into something new until you have gotten rid of something old.

Never expand into a new area until you have divested yourself of something in an older area.

What Should You Downsize, Discontinue, or Eliminate?

What are your key weaknesses? There are many parts of your business where you are active, yet you can never become the market leader in those areas. The cost of achieving market dominance is too high and/or your competition is too deeply entrenched with high-quality products and services.

One of the keys to focus and concentration is for you to have the foresight and courage to abandon certain products, services, and markets where you cannot achieve superiority. As Jack Welch famously said, "If you don't have a competitive advantage, don't compete."

His revolutionary strategic directive for GE was: "We will be number one or number two in every market, or we will abandon that market completely and focus on those markets where we can be number one or number two."

Admitting that you have both strengths and weaknesses in any area is an important step forward. Deciding to withdraw from or abandon a market where you cannot achieve victory is often the most intelligent strategic decision of all.

The Law of the Excluded Alternative

The Law of the Excluded Alternative says that "doing one thing means not doing all other things that you could be doing at the same time."

This means that whatever you choose to do, you are simultaneously choosing *not to do* anything else at that moment, or with that same amount of money. Sometimes, what you choose not to do is absolutely essential so that you are able to concentrate your powers where the greatest success is possible.

Managerial Ego

Businesses sometimes fail because of managerial ego. This happens when the decision maker invests his or her ego in a course of action that is not working, in a person who obviously cannot do the job, or in a product or service that is not selling.

When companies invest in managerial ego, they often take their best salespeople, their best marketing people, and their biggest advertising budgets and focus them on selling a product or service that is no longer successful or, even worse, has never been successful. But because somebody thought up this product and gave it the go-ahead, resources are wasted.

There's a saying: "If the horse is dead, get off!"

This maxim follows the Law of Holes: "If you find yourself in one, stop digging." The solution is not to dig the hole of failure and frustration deeper, but to begin digging somewhere else—and to begin doing or trying a different course of action.

FOURTEEN

Zero-Based Thinking

ZERO-BASED THINKING is one of the most powerful thinking tools you can use in strategic planning and throughout your career. The concept comes from zero-based accounting, where you draw a line under each item at the end of each accounting period and ask, "Rather than determining how much more or less we should spend in this area, should we be spending money in this area at all?"

In zero-based thinking, you use the same approach. You stand back and look at every part of your business and personal life and ask the question, "If I was not now doing this, knowing what I now know, would I get involved in this area again?"

We call this a KWINK (Knowing What I Now Know) analysis. Knowing what I now know, is there anything that I am doing today that I wouldn't get into again today if I had to do it over? In times of turbulence and rapid change, there is almost always one such example in your business or personal life. Often, there are several examples. There are many things that you are doing today that you would not start up again today if you had to do it over.

Beware the Comfort Zone

One of the greatest enemies of success is the "comfort zone." People become comfortable doing certain things in a certain way and then they resist any change. This resistance to change keeps people doing the wrong things, even when they know they are wrong, long after they should have stopped and tried something new.

Creating the future often means abandoning the *past*. Starting something new usually means that you have to stop something *old*. Getting into something for the first time usually means that you have to get out of other things to free up time and resources. Zero-based thinking is an essential tool to keep your mental decks cleared and to free up your thinking for the future.

Ask the Key Questions

When we do strategic planning for organizations, the first exercise we engage in is to go through the business systematically with this KWINK analysis:

1. Is there anything in your business that, knowing what you now know, you would not start up again today if you had to do it over?

2. Is there any product or service that you would not bring to the market again today, knowing what you now know?

3. Is there any business process, investment, or methodology that, knowing what you now know, you would not start up again today?

4. Is there any person in your business that, knowing what you now know, you would not have in your business if you had to do it over?

5. Is there any investment of time, money, or emotion that you have made or are currently making that, knowing what you now know, you would not make again today?

Determine Your Sunk Costs

There is a principle in accounting called a "sunk cost," which refers to a cost where the money is gone *forever*. It can never be recouped. It is like an anvil thrown off a ship in the middle of the ocean. It is sunk, gone forever, and cannot be retrieved.

Many expenses or investments of time or money in business are sunk costs. They are gone forever. The problem occurs when people continue to "throw good money after bad." They continue to invest time, money, and resources in a product, service, or area of activity in an effort to somehow recoup the amount they have already invested. But this is not possible. The money, time, or emotion is gone forever. It is a sunk cost.

Your job is to focus on the opportunities of tomorrow rather than allowing yourself to become preoccupied with the problems or bad decisions of the past. Your job is to think about the *future*, which you can control and do something about, rather than think about past events over which you have no control and cannot change.

Right or Wrong Decisions

What percentage of your decisions in business do you think will turn out to be wrong in the fullness of time? According to an American Management Association study and interviews with thousands of managers, fully 70 percent of business decisions turn out to be wrong over time. They may be a little bit wrong, a lot wrong, or completely disastrous.

That means you will probably be wrong 70 percent or more of the time. Remember, 70 percent is an average. Some people are above and some people are below this average.

One of the most important strategies for success in business is the decision to cut your losses. When you realize that you have made a bad decision, instead of pouring more money and resources into it in an attempt to recoup your losses, accept that you have made a bad decision, cut your losses, and move on. Practice zero-based thinking.

How Can You Tell?

How can you tell if you are dealing with a zero-based thinking situation? Simple: stress! Whenever you experience chronic stress—stress that does not go away, stress that preoccupies you and jumps up in your conversation, often keeping you awake at night—you are probably facing a zero-based thinking situation.

Your job is to have the *courage* necessary to face the situation honestly and do what you know you have to do. Don't play games with your own mind. Do not wish or hope that things will get better or that the problem will go away. Hope is not a strategy.

Instead, look at the stressful situation directly and ask, "If I was not now in this situation, knowing what I now know, would I get into it again today?"

If the answer is "No!" then the next question is, "How do I get out of this situation, and how fast?"

It Is Too Late

Here is the discovery. If and when you admit that you would not get into a particular situation again if you had to do it over, it is already too late to save the situation. It is over. Nothing can be done. It has become a sunk cost. The only question now is, how long will you wait to end this situation, and how much are you willing to pay in additional time, money, and emotion?

There is a Turkish proverb that says, "No matter how long you have gone down the wrong road, turn back."

Have the courage and honesty to practice zero-based thinking in every part of your life, and then to follow where your answer leads you. If a person or a product has not worked out, and it is clear that the situation is not going to get any better, cut your losses. End the situation and move on.

Take control of your life and your future. Make a decision. But don't hope and pray that somehow the situation will reverse itself and get better. This virtually never happens.

FIFTEEN

Take the Offensive

ALEXANDER ALMOST always fought against enemies with superior forces. He could not take a defensive position and wait for the enemy to surround and overlap his smaller army. To control the battlefield, he had to always think in terms of attack, of going on the offensive and taking the battle to the enemy.

In business, the strategy of the offensive requires that you continually bring out newer, better, faster, cheaper, and easier-to-use products and services. You introduce new technologies and new methods of marketing and selling. You continually change your pricing strategies and your cost structures. You form joint ventures and strategic alliances with other companies and organizations that can give you entry into different markets and enable you to outcompete your competitors.

Business Model Innovation

One of the most exciting areas of business thought today revolves around business model innovation. Many companies are still trying to survive and thrive using a business model that may have been appropriate a few years ago but that no longer works.

What is your business model today, and is it the appropriate model for your business in the current environment?

There is a simple way that you can test whether your business model is appropriate for today. It is leading to *continuous, consistent, and predictable growth in sales and profitability*. If your business is continuing to grow in a healthy way, your business model is probably appropriate. If your business is not growing in a healthy and consistent way, it may be time to question your business model.

A Better Way: Free Product

Instead of investing your ego in the way things are being done now, always be open to the possibility that there could be a better way. A useful exercise is to think about doing things exactly the opposite of what you are doing today. This opens your mind to a whole range of possibilities that you might not have seen before.

In his book *Free: The Future of a Radical Price*, author Chris Anderson points out that sometimes the very best way to sell more of your product at higher prices is to give all or part of it away at no charge to attract customers and to demonstrate the attractiveness of your offerings.

Give It Away?

Gary Vaynerchuk's 2014 book *Jab, Jab, Jab, Right Hook* shows how companies, especially Internet-based companies, can develop business and develop rapidly by offering three free products in a row before offering a product for sale.

For people and companies used to charging from the first customer decision, the idea of offering free products or services to build credibility and confidence in a highly competitive market may seem a bit radical. Nonetheless, more and more companies are generating millions and millions of dollars in sales by using the "give to get" model.

Take the Lead on Quality

In a 2013 *Inc.* magazine study of the 500 fastest-growing small and medium-size businesses in America, the researchers concluded that the best place to invest money to grow your business is back into improving the quality of your product or service in some way. This would have more predictable and consistent effects on increased sales and profitability than anything else that you could do.

The fact is that quality is an *offensive* marketing strategy. Quality is a profit strategy. The quality leaders in every field are also the most profitable companies in every field. Today, the highest-grossing retail store in the world per square foot is Tiffany & Co. The second is Apple. Both are the recognized quality leaders in their industries. Where do you rank?

Reinvent Yourself

In his book *The Road to Reinvention*, author Josh Linkner shows how companies can grab the offensive by constantly reinventing themselves. This is not just having a fallback plan—it's taking the initiative and changing your company before your competitors have even managed to get you in their sights. Linkner gives eight principles to follow if you want to successfully reinvent your company:

1. *Let go of the past.* What's done is done. You may take some lessons from the past, but then let it go.

2. *Encourage courage.* Don't punish your employees or managers when they want to try something different. Reward them!

3. *Embrace failure.* People will never try something new if they are afraid of failing. It's through failures that you learn the lessons that build the success of the future.

4. *Do the opposite.* I already mentioned this strategy before, and Linkner agrees. Be contrarian. Do the unexpected. You'll be surprised at what happens.

5. *Imagine the possibilities.* Close your eyes. Forget about the roadblocks and barriers—put them out of your mind. What do you see?

6. *Put yourself out of business.* A lot of companies are afraid to cannibalize their products. They think that if we offer this new product, customers will stop buying our old product! This is a trap, because if you can make a new product to replace your old one, so can your competition. Cannibalize your products . . . or someone else will.

7. *Reject limits.* There will always be naysayers. Nobody has done anything of significance without somebody saying it can't be done. Decide that the limits don't apply to you.

8. *Aim beyond.* Look forward; look beyond what's happening now to what will be happening in the future. Anticipate trends.

After the Fire

Think of your business as a bundle of resources and capabilities. Those resources and capabilities can be used to create and sell many products and services—and not necessarily the ones you are selling today!

Imagine that you arrived at work one morning and your company had burned down overnight. Luckily, none of your staff members were in the building, but everything else is gone.

You now must start the business almost from scratch. This leaves you with a number of questions to answer:

- Which products and services do you want to start making and selling, and which products, knowing what you know now, would you decide not to produce

- Which customers do you want to try to reach, and which customers, knowing what you know now, would you decide not to try to win back?

- Which employees would you take with you to the new business, and which employees would you decline to keep?

Now that you are in this starting-from-scratch mind-set, don't wait for the fire. Make the move and surprise your competitors with a reinvented company.

SIXTEEN

Flexibility Wins

IN CHAPTER TWO, I talked about the principle of maneuver, which in business means maintaining the flexibility to innovate and respond quickly to whatever happens in your environment.

The principle of maneuver requires that you continually anticipate what *might* happen. You develop fallback positions. You prepare to be able to move forward, backward, and sideways in the market, if necessary. You resolve never to get locked into a single plan with no flexibility or no other choice. You continually keep your options open and develop new options.

Avoid Limited Thinking

Darius had only one plan. His plan was that the chariots would break through and he would demoralize the Macedonian army. Then his men would march forward and envelop the demoralized Macedonian troops, overwhelming them and wiping them out. He would win. But when the chariots didn't work, Darius had no fallback plan. It cost him the greatest empire that the world had ever seen to that date.

Alexander had a fallback plan if the chariots of Darius were able to get through to his army. His men were prepared to quickly maneuver to form columns and create a broad passageway so that the chariots and riders could run through into the back of his army where his special troops were waiting to chop them to pieces.

Prepare Contingency Plans

Royal Dutch Shell is one of the most successful companies in the world. It has oil and gas extraction activities in a hundred countries, combined with pipelines to get the gas and oil to ships and refineries. It has ships to transport the fuel to markets and even gas stations blanketing the countries in which Shell operates, to sell finished products to the driver at the pump.

Royal Dutch Shell is also famous for its "contingency planning." Over the years, the company has developed more than 600 contingency plans for any setback or emergency that could occur anywhere in the world that would affect its operations in any way. No matter what happens in terms of wars, revolutions, terrorist attacks, the closing of shipping routes, the fall of governments, the abrogation of contracts with governments to cut off supplies of gas, oil, or markets in a particular area, Shell has developed a plan.

Flexible Operations

It used to be that the strategy for growing operations went in only one direction: scaling up. Scaling up was the best way to get the most productivity and to reduce unit costs. Bigger was better. Ten 100-ton dump trucks using ten drivers carry the same amount of load as 100 ten-ton dump trucks requiring 100 drivers! So scale up to those 100-ton dump trucks as soon as you can.

At least, that was the old way of thinking. But according to professors Garrett van Ryzin of Columbia Business School and Klaus Lackner of Columbia University's School of Engineering and Applied Science, the old way of thinking may not be the most efficient. New automation and communication technology are changing the rules. Now a large number of small units may be better than a small number of large units because they introduce a whole new level of flexibility.

Here's an example. Chlorine is a chemical that's widely used in industry. The problem is that it is also very dangerous to transport. Under the old rules, manufacturers would achieve economies of scale by building large chlorine plants to save money on labor and other costs. But automation and technology means that today, labor costs in those plants are low. On the other hand, a fewer number of plants means dangerous transportation across long distances. So instead of building huge plants, chlorine manufacturers are building a lot of small chlorine plants that are automated and remotely monitored.

Going Small

Van Ryzin and Lackner list the benefits of rejecting the old economies of scale strategy in industrial production:

- *Risk reduction.* Large-scale industrial disasters are less likely.

- *Financial flexibility.* Large plants are often running at below capacity. Build a small plant. Then when you need it, build another small plant.

- *Operating flexibility.* If your needs go down, it's easy to just take a small plant completely offline. If you have just a few large plants, you'll have to keep them open.

- *Geographic flexibility.* You can disperse a number of small plants to locations close to supply and demand sources.

Going small and flexible when everyone else in your industry is still thinking bigger is better is a major way to outmaneuver your competitors.

SEVENTEEN

Create New Markets

HERE'S A RISKY strategy that can lead to great rewards: creating a new market. The best way to create a new market is to find the problem first. There are problems for which there are no solutions. Your solution is the new market. Minivans fill our roads today, but it wasn't so long ago that the market for minivans didn't exist. Chrysler, recognizing that its gas-guzzling full-size vans were becoming less popular, saw the need for a scaled-down version of vans. A new and very profitable market was born.

Four Paths

In his book *Creating and Dominating New Markets*, Peter Meyer gives four paths for creating and dominating new markets.

Path 1. Create a new product for an unknown customer set. This is the riskiest of the paths. You are creating a new product for a new customer set. You have no experience or knowledge on which to build; you are starting with a clean slate. It's not impossible to succeed if you hit on the right problem. When Netscape created a web browser, it created a new product for unknown customers—most people weren't using the Internet at the time. Would there be enough people to eventually use the Internet to make a browser profitable? Did Netscape create the right product for browsing through the Internet? In hindsight, the answers are obvious, but at the beginning of the process, Netscape had to make the investments with little idea of the outcome.

Path 2. Create a new product for a known customer set. Path 2 has a major advantage over path 1 because you have some knowledge and experience to build on, specifically your history with the customer. You know or have a good idea of what customers want or will want.

Path 3. Create a known product for a known customer set. While this may seem the easiest path, it is actually quite difficult because to create a new market, you have to break from what's been done in the past. Often, companies are not really creating a new market; they are only creating a variation of an existing market—basically doing nothing more than a line extension.

Path 4. Create a known product for an unknown customer set. Here, like with path 2, you have the advantage of building on some knowledge but with room to innovate. As a result, the risks are reduced. You know that the product has sold to previous customers, so the chances are greater that it will succeed with new customers.

The most important success factor in creating new markets is to ask your customers. The goal is not to ask them about products but about problems. If you ask about products, they'll frame the problem in the context of those products. Your goal, however, is find ideas for new products. Let customers describe what they think would be the best solution to their problems; those solutions will point to new products or services.

Key Success Factors

Creating new markets is not a strategy for those looking for easy wins. But you can increase your chances for success, according to Meyer, if you follow these guidelines:

■ *Let the customer drive.* Customer-driven markets have a greater chance of succeeding than vendor-driven markets because customers usually know what they want . . . and what they don't want!

■ *Take the easier paths.* If you can, go for paths 2 or 4. Build on something already in place (a known product or a known customer set).

■ *Don't chase every opportunity.* Not every opportunity is going to be worth the attention, especially if it is diluting your efforts.

■ *Build cross-functional teams.* A new market will never be the purview of just one function. Everyone will need to be involved.

Blue Ocean Strategy

The blue ocean strategy concept, developed by professors W. Chan Kim and Renée Mauborgne, is based on the idea that most companies battle in a part of the ocean that is filled with competitors and the (metaphorically speaking) bloody competition makes that part of the ocean red. All of today's industries are red oceans. Instead of fighting the competition, a better strategy is to create your own market: to find a blue ocean where there are no competitors.

To do this, Kim and Mauborgne present different tools and concepts in their famous book, *Blue Ocean Strategy*. At the heart of this strategy is "value innovation," which they describe as the "simultaneous pursuit of differentiation and low cost." Differentiation is what customers want; value, in the customer's eyes, is the "utility" of the product minus its price. Low cost is what companies want; value for companies is the price minus the cost to make the product.

Value innovation lowers costs by eliminating factors that the industry competes on, but increases value by creating factors the industry does not compete on. For example, Canon's traditional competitors sold large, durable copiers to corporate purchasers. Canon had the idea to change the buyer; instead of focusing on corporate purchasers, it decided to focus on the people who used the copiers, the administrative assistants. Suddenly the key competitive factors changed . . . and the desktop copier industry—a sparkling blue ocean—was born.

EIGHTEEN

Choose Your Competition

CHOOSING YOUR strategy means choosing your competitor. Your competitor determines your level of sales, your prices, your profitability, your market share, and how fast or how slow you grow.

In warfare they say that no strategy is possible without consideration of the enemy—knowing who the enemy is and what the enemy is likely to do. It is the same in business. In Michael Porter's work on competitive advantage at Harvard, he points out that competitive response to your marketing activities, or what your competitors are likely to do, must be a primary consideration in all of your strategic planning.

Identify Your Competitors

Who or what is your competitor for your product or service today? Who are your main competitors? Who are your smaller competitors?

What *else* is your competitor? Since you are asking a potential customer to give you a certain amount of money in order to acquire a certain benefit or advantage, where else can your potential customer spend that same amount of money to get an equal or better advantage or benefit? This is an extremely important question.

When I was doing work with Carnival Cruise Lines, I asked the company's executives what other cruise lines they competed against. They explained to me that they did not compete against other cruise lines. The cruise business was growing and continued to grow as more and more people took more and more cruises worldwide.

Their major competitor, they explained, was "land-based vacations," which were the major substitute or alternative to ship-based vacations. Their job was to position a cruise as being superior to a vacation on land anywhere.

Any Alternate Use of Funds

Any alternate expenditure of the amount of money that you request from your customer is also a competitor. As Sam Walton once said, "We have only one boss. That is the customer. And customers can fire us at any time just by deciding to spend their money somewhere else."

Where else could a potential customer of yours spend the same amount of money to get an equal or greater level of benefit or satisfaction? How can you position yourself so that the product or service you offer is a superior choice to a customer who has the option to spend that money somewhere else?

Choose Your Competitor

Choosing your product or service means choosing your competitor as well. Often, you can change your business by deciding to compete against another organization. Changing your competitor can lead to changing your business completely.

Once you have identified your major and minor competitors, sit down and analyze both their strengths and weaknesses. Analyze your strengths and weaknesses. Where are you vulnerable to your competitors? Where are they vulnerable to you?

Position Yourself as the Superior Choice

How could you position your products or services in such a way that they are clearly superior to those of your competitors? What could you do more of or less of to improve the attractiveness of your offering in comparison to your competitors? What could you start doing (or stop doing) to make your products or services more appealing than your competitors?

Resolve to be objective in answering these questions. Don't just tell yourself that you are better than your competitors. Sit down and write out carefully itemized answers to these questions. Then do market research among customers and prospective customers to make sure that you are correct in your conclusions.

The only real test of the accuracy of your conclusions is a market test. You only know for sure that you are doing and offering the right combination of benefits and prices when you enjoy a steady increase in sales and profitability in your business.

NINETEEN

Engage the Entire Company

WHEN IMPLEMENTING strategy, the entire company must be working together seamlessly. Everybody must believe in the strategy and know what it means for their work and activities. All the goals and processes of the different parts of the company must be aligned. This is the principle of concerted action. Alexander's army was known for being a united fighting force, the soldiers always ready to support each other in battle.

In contrast, the army of Darius was made up of many disparate sources, in terms of customs, languages, military traditions, levels of training, and officers—some of whom did not speak the languages of the others around them. When the army started to come apart, there was no team cohesion or unity of command to hold them together as a single fighting force. The result was disastrous.

The same unity on behalf of the whole must be found in your company. Everyone must be dedicated to making the strategy work—and that means all of your employees must be dedicated to helping each other in achieving their goals.

Because they so readily support each other and are completely dedicated and loyal to the company, employees in a united company form a "fighting force" that gives them a tremendous advantage over competitors in their markets. Along with high levels of teamwork, they are fully engaged in their work. As a result, they are more creative and innovative. They have higher morale and they get along better with each other. They have a greater esprit de corps.

Business Units Working Together

More than likely, you have different business units, business divisions, or even subsidiaries in your company. A corporate strategy can get tripped up if there is poor integration among the different parts of your structure. In the book *Making Strategy Work*, Wharton professor Lawrence G. Hrebiniak describes three tasks or decisions that you want to make concerning integration.

First, what kind of *interdependence* should you have among units? There are three kinds of interdependence. Pooled interdependence is the lowest level of interdependence. There's little coordination. Units are self-contained and self-directed. Sequential interdependence requires a little more coordination and cooperation because what happens in one unit then affects another unit. Reciprocal interdependence is the highest level of connection and cooperation. Every unit interacts and depends on other units.

Second, how are you making sure units are sharing information and transferring knowledge? It's hard to overstress the importance of communication. Know whom you're talking to and make sure that they understand and appreciate the knowledge that they are receiving. Sometimes, technical issues are not fully explained. Other times, it can be a cultural problem.

Third, have you clarified responsibility and accountability? If people don't know what they're responsible for, don't expect them to do their jobs. Coordination and cooperation are not possible without responsibility and accountability.

Motivate Employees

To engage all of your employees in the company's strategy, you have to set the right incentives. The keys to good incentives, according to Hrebiniak, are incentives that do not demotivate people (do your incentives spark a need for achievement?); incentives that fuel and guide motivation but don't try to create it (that doesn't work); incentives that are tied to strategic objectives; and incentives that reward the right things.

It's one thing to motivate employees and managers, but you also need to have a system of controls, says Hrebiniak. Controls are going to give you the feedback you need about how well your people are actively supporting the strategy. To make sure controls are working effectively:

- Reward the doers.

- Face the brutal facts.

- Clarify responsibility and accountability.

- Get timely and pertinent information.

- Step up to your leadership responsibilities, modeling the right behaviors and establishing an honest relationship with your subordinates.

- Conduct a strategy review, which clarifies the strategy and sets execution-related objectives.

Embedding the Strategy Throughout the Company

Your goal is to embed the strategy in the company. This means that most of your employees fully understand, accept, and support the strategy.

Some business leaders try to embed the strategy by "cascading" the message about strategy down the organizational chart. CEOs talk directly to their team of top managers, who in turn talk to mid-level managers, who talk to their lower-level direct reports, who talk to supervisors, and on down the line until you get to the frontline employees.

To get buy-in from employees, do more than cascade the message down to your people. Talk to them directly. Research by professor Charles Galunic, based on 60,000 responses to a survey sent to more than 350 companies, shows that employees don't really believe or buy into strategy that's communicated by their supervisors. They want to hear the strategy directly from top management. They also want to know that their feedback and thoughts are being heard by top managers.

Professor Galunic gives two reasons direct communication from senior managers is important. First, strategic goals and direction aren't always easy to communicate, and as the strategy gets passed from one person to another, it is likely to become more confused and garbled. Remember: Clarity is essential. Don't muddle the message by having it go through a string of managers.

Second, people are going to take the talk from top managers more seriously. If the CEO is taking the time to speak with frontline employees directly, those employees know that the subject is important.

TWENTY

Organizational Structure Makes a Difference

HOW IS YOUR company structured? Are decisions centralized or are they mostly decentralized to business units and subsidiaries? Do you have operations scattered around the globe or are you grouped in one location, with everyone under the same roof—from production to sales and marketing?

When business leaders think of strategy, they think a lot about product development and sales and marketing. But the structure of your company can make a big difference in the successful implementation of your strategy.

Wharton professor Lawrence Hrebiniak writes about the importance of connecting strategy with structure. If your structure is not aligned with your strategy, even the best strategy can fail.

Hrebiniak asks: What parts of your strategy are going to impact the structure you choose? And what parts of your structure are important in the execution of your strategy?

For example, if you make a commodity product, your strategy is going to be based on becoming a low-cost producer. In this case, your structure is intended to achieve economies of scale and scope. What can you standardize? How can you reduce costs? What tasks can you make repeatable?

If your strategy is to be a specialist company, making something for a certain type of customer, or if you have a geographic focus, then you probably want to be decentralized into different business units. But you still need to coordinate across your decentralized units.

If you have a differentiation strategy (see Chapter Ten), then you should create different business divisions for your high-end or low-end products.

For global operations, your structure must be able to support your worldwide products, but at the same time you have to take into account different geographical preferences. In this case, a matrix organization is a good structure: You can focus horizontally on your products and focus vertically on the different geographic markets.

The Centralization Decision

The structure question that most companies have to ask themselves is: Do you centralize or not? Do you push decisions down the organization to your divisions or business units, or do you keep them at headquarters?

A *McKinsey Quarterly* article identified three fundamental questions to ask when making the centralization decision. If there is a "no" answer to all three of these questions, the company should not centralize. One "yes" answer, however, is all that's needed to move forward with centralization.

1. *Is centralization mandated?* In other words, is it required? There are certain decisions that by law have to be made by the CEO. But for most decisions, who handles the decision is up to the company.

2. *Does centralization create significant value?* If you are going to take something away from your business unit heads, there should be a good financial reason. The *McKinsey Quarterly* article suggests 10 percent return on the decision.

3. *Are the risks low?* If you've answered "no" to the first two questions, then the only reason to move forward with centralization is because there's little risk of the typical bad side effects of centralization (e.g., stifled initiative or the inability to tailor products for local markets).

Strategy is formulated at the top, but it must be adopted by everyone throughout the organization. In the previous chapter, I noted that it's best that top management communicate directly with all levels of the organization. But when it comes to implementing the strategy, centralizing decisions related to that strategy should be done very carefully. Unless you can answer "yes" to the three previous questions, put the day-to-day implementation of your strategy in the hands of your division and business unit leaders. But stay in close contact in case the strategy goes off the track for whatever reason.

TWENTY-ONE

The Five Phases of Strategy Formulation and Implementation

BENJAMIN TREGOE, cofounder of the global consulting company Kepner-Tregoe, and the firm's president Mike Freedman developed the five phases of strategic formulation and implementation. These five phases give you a good overview of the strategic journey.

The first phase is *strategic intelligence gathering and analysis.* As I've said before, strategy is about asking the right questions. In Freedman and Tregoe's first phase, you have to first know which questions to ask, and then go and find the data that will help you answer the questions. There is more data available than ever before. The trick today is to know what data to use and what to ignore.

You should find the data that is going to help you figure out the trends and assumptions about your business. Any other data should be ignored.

When thinking about the future of your business, start with your external environment. What are the trends in society, government, politics, technology, and the economy that are relevant to you? Next look at the trends affecting your key players—your customers and suppliers. Look at your value chain. How will it differ in the future? What key success factors are going to be required? How will your industry change?

Look Inside

Next, pull together the data that helps you see the trends that relate to your company's internal factors. What sells well, what doesn't, and why? Which customers and markets are you successful with, and why?

Dissect your past strategies. Which strategies have worked and which haven't? Which strategies were supported by your employees and other stakeholders, and which weren't? How well did you implement previous strategies?

The goal is to get all the data you need to build the foundation of the remaining four steps of strategy formulation and implementation. In this phase, you have the information to put forward some assumptions about what your internal and external environments will look like in the future—and what you need to do to succeed. You'll be able to identify potential problems on the road, but also potential opportunities.

The second phase is *strategy formulation*—that is, you choose the strategy you are going to follow. Start with the time frame. A strategy should have an endpoint. When you talk about the future, what time period are you talking about?

Your time frame is going to depend on forces inside and outside the organization. New regulations or changes in your industry are going to push you to achieve your strategies within a certain time frame.

A second defining factor are the basic beliefs of your organization. Your strategy must take place in the context of the company's values and beliefs. Beliefs guide your organization's day-to-day behavior and practices and build your organization's culture.

Driving Force

Once you have the parameters of a time frame and know your basic beliefs, you can now decide on your driving force. The driving force is at the heart of Kepner-Tregoe's formulation phase. It's the driving force that tells you what products and services you are going to offer and what markets you will (or will not) serve. I described the driving force in detail in Chapter Nine.

Once you've chosen your driving force, you have to now align your products and services and your target markets with that driving force. You will not want to attack both new products and new markets at the same time. Let your driving force set your new priorities while maintaining your successful areas. The product or service driving force means you have successful products or services. Growth will come by selling those products in new markets. The market needs driving force requires you to focus on your markets and perhaps find new products or services.

The next step is to lay out the financial targets for the strategy. What do you expect in terms of ROI or profits? What will be your revenues?

The Product/Market Matrix

Close out phase 2 (strategy formulation) by creating a product/market matrix that lists current, modified, and new products horizontally across the top, and all the current, modified, and new markets vertically for each of those products. In each box decide on the degree of emphasis (from "high" to "not applicable" or "don't pursue"). You now have a roadmap for your strategic profile.

Then move on to the third phase: *strategy master project planning*. In this phase, you'll create a list of potential key projects (including existing key projects such as upgrading IT) based on the strategic profile and product/market matrix from phase 2, then analyze and prioritize every potential project. This pool of projects is your action plan for the strategy.

Strategy Implementation

Phase 4 of Freedman and Tregoe's five phases is *strategic implementation*. This is the hard part. Pay attention to the details as you roll out projects (and add more projects as more resources become available). Everything is going to impact implementation. Do you have the right organization structure (see Chapter Twenty)? Is the information reaching the people it needs to reach?

One important issue to examine in this phase is culture. Are your culture and strategy aligned? Do the values and beliefs in your company support the decisions you've made about products, markets, and financial goals? Look at your performance goals. Are you rewarding people in a way that will encourage them to achieve the strategic goals you've set?

Communication is the final piece of the implementation puzzle (see Chapter Nineteen). If you are not communicating the strategy successfully, the strategy will die on the vine.

Monitor, Review, Updates

Phase 5 entails continuously *monitoring, reviewing,* and *updating* your strategy. Never let up. Your strategy may be well on its way and then could be derailed because you are not paying close attention. Are people achieving their strategic goals? Are the strategic projects accomplished in a timely manner, and are they yielding the expected results? Things change. If something in the environment changes, you may have to revisit some of your earlier strategic decisions. Also, some of the assumptions made when you were creating the strategy might prove to be wrong. In that case, you need to adjust your strategy or maybe go in a different direction.

Remember: The work of a strategist is never done.

INDEX